Your First Keyboard Method

Mary Thompson

EXCLUSIVELY DISTRIBUTED BY

HAL•LEONARD®

Music and text setting by Mary Thompson
Illustrations by Nigel Hooper
Cover design by Ian Butterworth

Order No. AM 945230
International Standard Book Number: 0.8256.1633.6

Contents

About Your First Keyboard Book

This book will help you to learn the
piano, or keyboard, in very easy stages.
You will find out the names of the notes,
and how they are written down. You will
also learn about some of the signs and
symbols used in music, the black keys,
and you will begin to play tunes with both
hands at the same time.

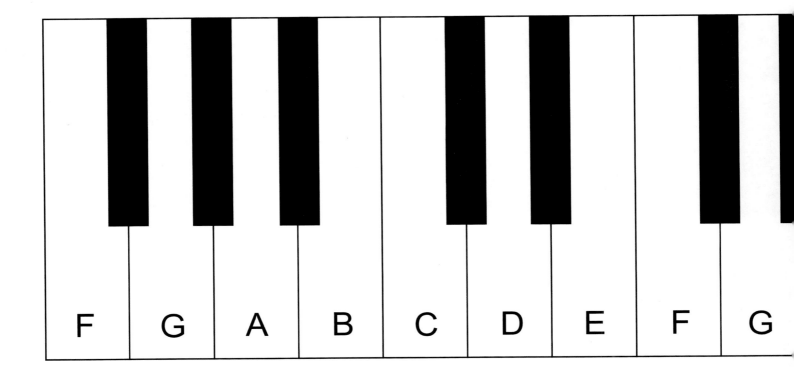

F G A B C D E F G

About Your Keyboard

Here you can see what your keyboard looks like. You make a sound by pressing the keys. The white keys are named after the first seven letters of the alphabet. The black keys are in groups of two and three.

The keys on the left side of the keyboard sound lower than the keys on the right. Try pressing some of the keys and listen to the sound they make.

Remember, if you are learning on an electronic keyboard, you will need to turn it on first!

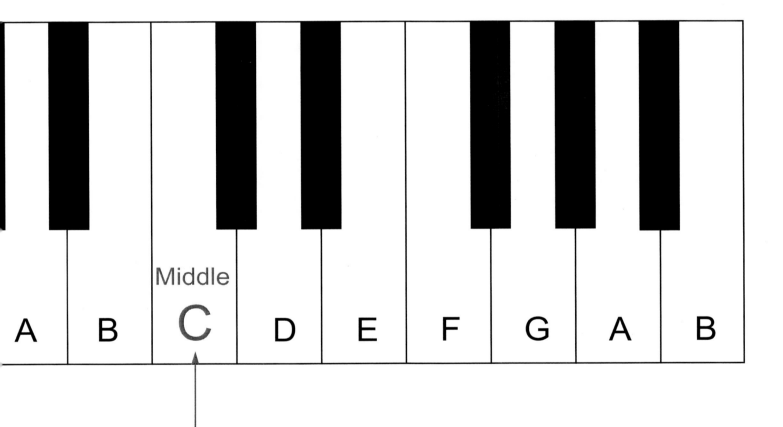

Middle C

A B C D E F G A B

The most important key for you to find is Middle C. This is the C nearest the middle of your keyboard.

Try to find Middle C on your keyboard. Then try to find some other Cs. They are always to the left of two black keys.

How Music Is Written Down

Music is written on a set of lines, called a *staff*. In piano and keyboard music, there is a separate staff for each hand to play.

At the beginning of each staff there is a sign called a *clef*. The *treble clef* is used for higher notes and the *bass clef* is used for lower notes. You can find out more about notes on the opposite page.

This is called a treble clef.

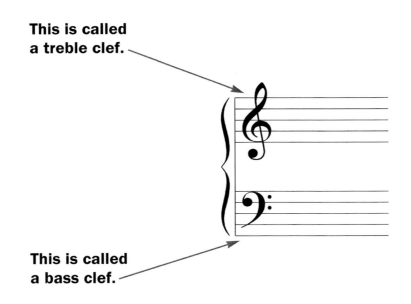

This is called a bass clef.

Play the music on the top staff with your right hand.

Play the music on the bottom staff with your left hand.

Musical Notes

When you write a story you use words to make up a sentence. In music, you use notes to make up a tune.

Each note has a name. The names of the notes are the same as the names of the keys on your keyboard.

You can see the names of the notes below.

Some notes go on the lines.

Others go in the spaces between the lines.

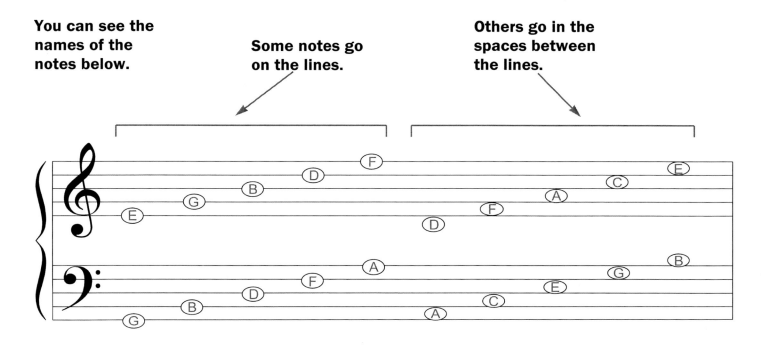

Remembering the Names of the Notes

To help you remember the names of the notes, you could make up some funny phrases.

Why not try making up some of your own? You could use the names of people you know.

Treble clef phrases

For the notes on the lines:

Every Great Big Dragon Flies

For the notes in the spaces:

Don't Forget Auntie Catches Everything

Bass clef phrases

For the notes on the lines:

Great Big Ducks From Alaska

For the notes in the spaces:

Auntie Catches Every Giant Bug

How Long Notes Last

Notes can last for different lengths. The length of a note is measured in steady counts, called *beats*. You have to count the number of beats very carefully as you play.

Whole Notes

A *whole note* is a long note. It lasts for four beats. So every time you play a whole note you need to count to four before playing the next note.

This is a whole note.

Splitting Music Up Into Sections

When you write a story you leave a space between each word. This makes it easier to read. Music is split up into short sections too. Each section is called a *bar*. The bars are separated by lines, called *barlines*.

At the beginning of the music there are numbers to tell you how many beats are in each bar. These numbers are called the *time signature*. Always look at the time signature before you start to play.

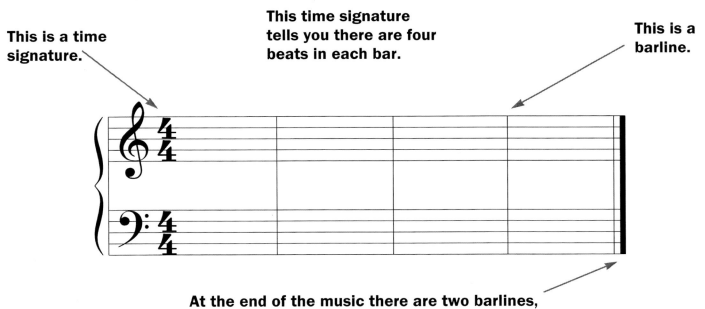

This is a time signature.

This time signature tells you there are four beats in each bar.

This is a barline.

At the end of the music there are two barlines, to let you know the music is finished.

Your First Note

The first note you are going to learn is Middle C. Here you can see where to find Middle C on your keyboard, and how it is written on the staff.

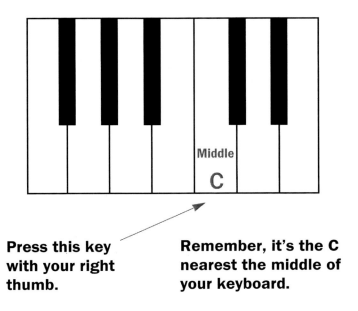

Middle

C

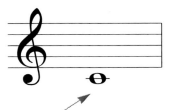

This is how Middle C is written for your right hand.

It has its own line, just below the staff.

Press this key with your right thumb.

Remember, it's the C nearest the middle of your keyboard.

Piggy in the Middle

Play the tune below with your right thumb. Press the key, count to four, then press the key again.

Try to count as evenly as you can.

Count: 1 2 3 4   1 2 3 4   1 2 3 4   1 2 3 4

Practice Hints

- Try clapping the rhythm before you start to play.

- Clap a little louder for the first beat of each bar.

- It might help to count out loud as you clap.

- Keep the key pressed down for the full four beats.

Which Fingers to Use

Each finger has a number. On the right you can see which numbers go with each finger on your right hand.

When you see a number above a note, this tells you which finger to use. For example, a number one tells you to play the note with your thumb.

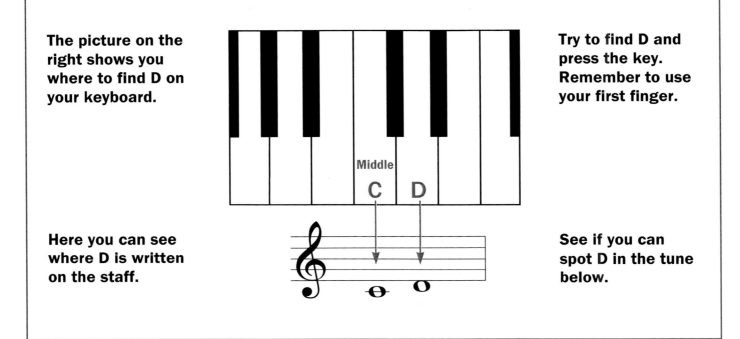

The picture on the right shows you where to find D on your keyboard.

Try to find D and press the key. Remember to use your first finger.

Middle C D

Here you can see where D is written on the staff.

See if you can spot D in the tune below.

Dozy D

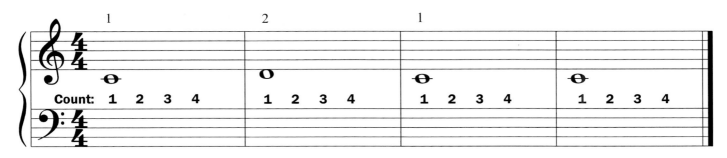

1   2   1

Count: 1 2 3 4   1 2 3 4   1 2 3 4   1 2 3 4

A Different Note Length

On page 8 you learned about whole notes.
On this page you will learn about notes
which last for two beats, called *half notes*.

If the time signature at the beginning of
the music is $\frac{4}{4}$, then you can fit two half
notes in each bar.

This is a half note.

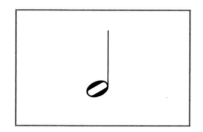

Two By Two

Remember, count two beats when you
play a half note and four beats when you
play a whole note. Try to count the beats
in your head if you can.

**Count the beats as
evenly as you can.**

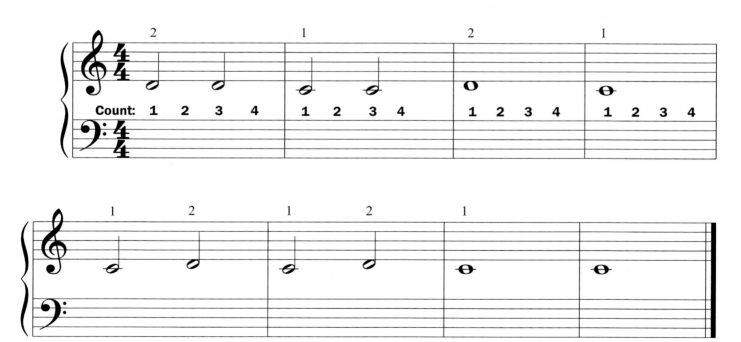

Another Note Length

So far you have learned about whole notes and half notes. On this page you will learn about *quarter notes,* which last for one beat.

If the time signature at the beginning of the music is $\frac{4}{4}$, then you can fit four quarter notes in each bar.

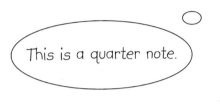

This is a quarter note.

Quarter Note Crazy

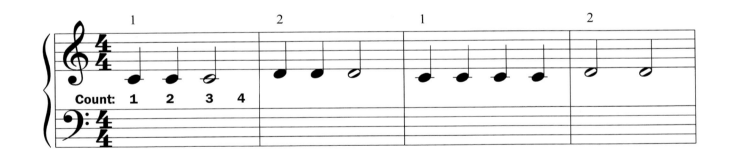

The picture on the right shows you where to find E on your keyboard.

Remember, the number 3 over a note tells you to use your middle finger.

Here you can see where E is written on the staff.

See if you can spot E in the tune below.

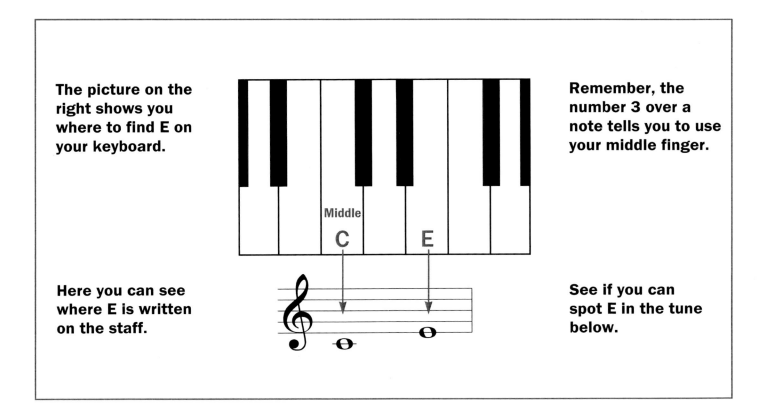

Merrily We Roll Along

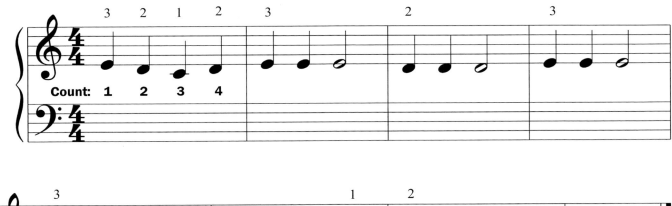

Using Your Left Hand

On this page you will learn some notes for your left hand to play. Like the right hand, each left-hand finger has a number. On the right you can see which number goes with each finger.

The picture on the right shows you where to find the notes on your keyboard.

Find the notes, then press the keys. Start with your left thumb on middle C.

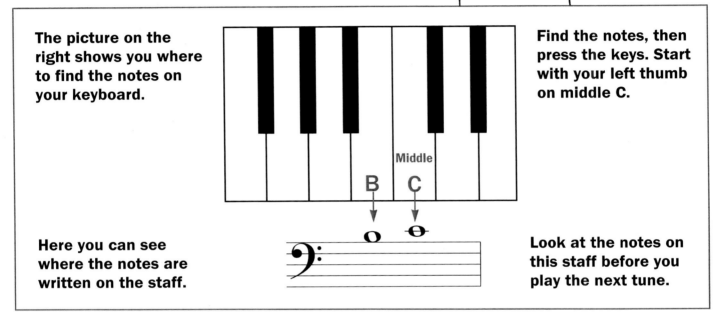

Here you can see where the notes are written on the staff.

Look at the notes on this staff before you play the next tune.

Moving On

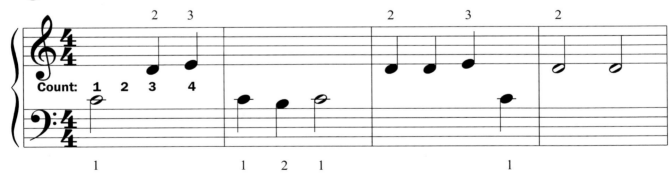

A New Time Signature

There is a new time signature in the tune below. It has a number three on top instead of a number four. This means there are three beats in each bar. The number four on the bottom tells you that a quarter note gets one beat.

Leftover Waltz

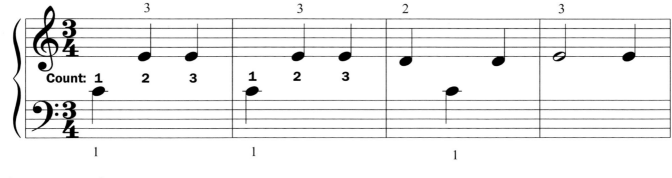

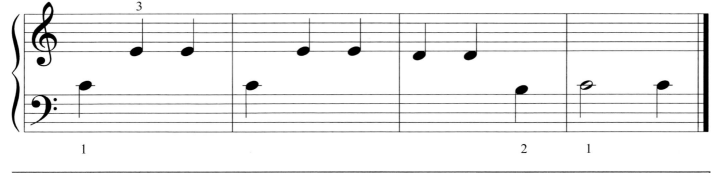

Practice Hints

- Before you start to play, make sure your arms and fingers are very relaxed.

- Start by playing something you can already play well. This will help to give you confidence when you play more difficult pieces.

- Practice for a few minutes each day, rather than for an hour once a week. You will remember more, the more often you play.

- When you play something new, try to play it all the way through, even if you make some mistakes.

Repeat Signs

There is a new sign at the end of the tune below. It is called a *repeat sign*. When you see this sign, go back to the beginning and play the music again. The second time you reach the repeat sign, stop playing.

Practice the tune below slowly at first, until you are sure of the notes. Then try playing it faster, bit by bit.

The picture on the right shows you where to find F on your keyboard.

Remember, a number 4 over a note tells you to use your fourth finger.

Here you can see where F is written on the staff.

See if you can spot F in the tune below.

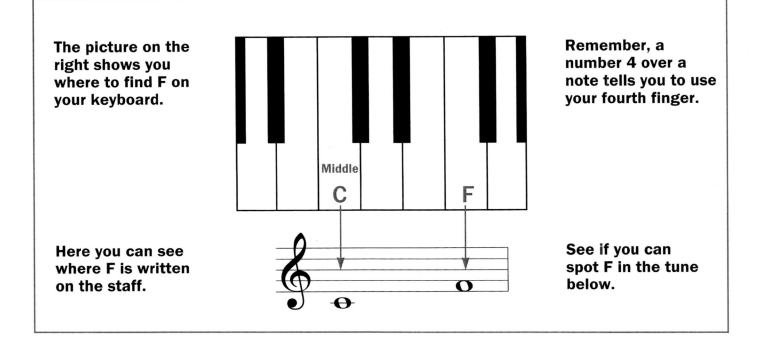

Playtime

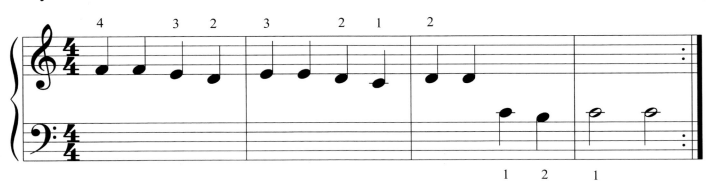

Playing Quietly

When you *see* the word piano, or the letter p, play the music quietly.

There are words in music that tell you how loudly or quietly to play. These words are in Italian, because the first printed music came from Italy. The Italian word for "quietly" is *piano*. Sometimes *piano* is shortened to ***p***.

To play notes quietly on a piano, press the keys very gently. If you are learning on an electronic keyboard, you can adjust the volume control so the sound is quieter.

Try playing a few notes. Press the keys hard for some, and more gently for others. Listen to how loud or quiet each note sounds.

Lullaby

There is a letter ***p*** at the beginning of this tune. Press the keys very gently all the way through. Remember to look at the time signature before you start to play.

Count three beats in every bar.

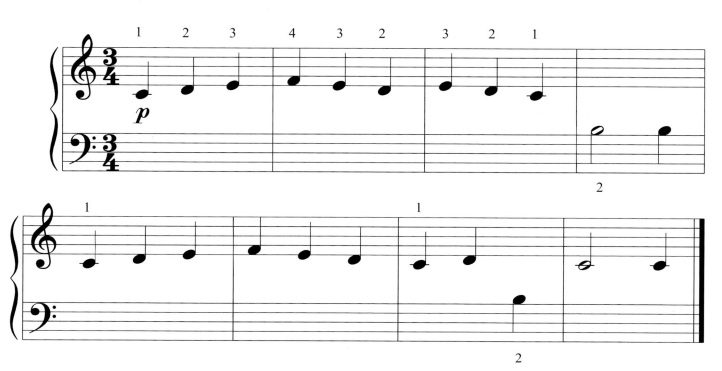

Music Quiz

On this page there are some questions about the things you have learned so far. The answers are all in this book, so you can check to see how many you get right.

1. How many beats do you count for this note?

2. What is the letter-name of this note?

3. What does this sign mean?

4. Which hand would you use to play this music?

5. What is the Italian word for "quietly?"

6. How many bars are there in this tune?

7. If the time signature is ¾, how many beats are there in each bar?

8. What is the letter-name of this note?

9. How many beats do you count for this note?

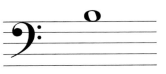

10. What does the letter *p* mean in music?

Notes You Have Learned So Far

Review and practice the notes you've learned to this point.

Playing Loudly

On page 17 you learned the Italian word *piano,* which means "quietly." Sometimes you have to play the music loudly. The Italian word for "loudly" is *forte.* The word *forte* is often shortened to *f*.

If you are learning on a piano, press the keys harder to play loudly. If you are learning on an electronic keyboard, you can adjust the volume control so the sound is louder.

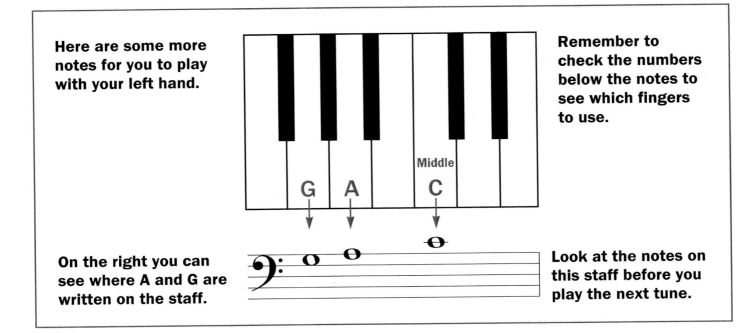

Here are some more notes for you to play with your left hand.

Remember to check the numbers below the notes to see which fingers to use.

On the right you can see where A and G are written on the staff.

Look at the notes on this staff before you play the next tune.

Left a Bit

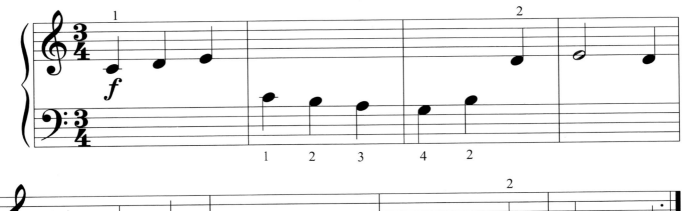

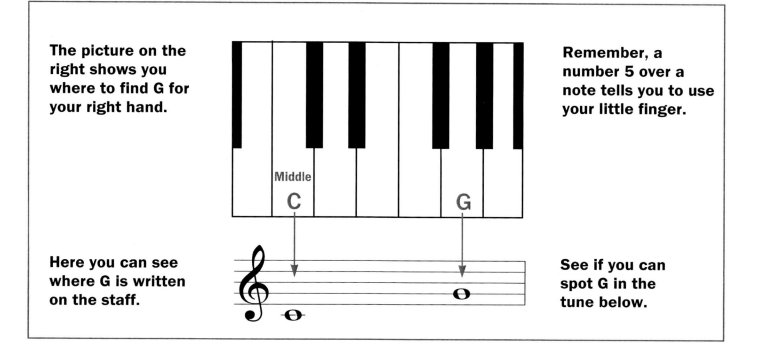

The picture on the right shows you where to find G for your right hand.

Remember, a number 5 over a note tells you to use your little finger.

Here you can see where G is written on the staff.

See if you can spot G in the tune below.

Marching On

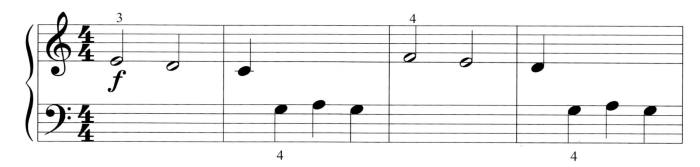

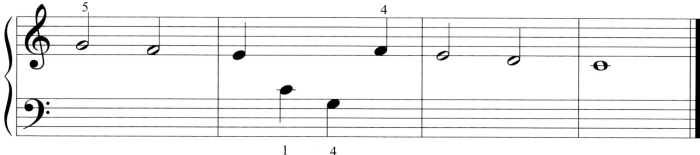

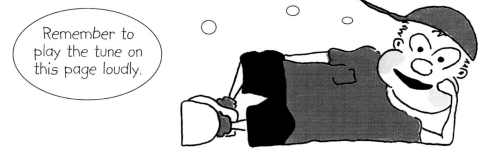

Remember to play the tune on this page loudly.

Dotted Notes

Sometimes there is a dot after a note. This makes the note last for one and a half times its normal length. For example, a half note lasts for two beats, so a half note with a dot after it lasts for three beats. When there is a dot after a note, it is called a *dotted note*.

This is a dotted half note.

Dot to Dot

Remember to play this tune quietly.

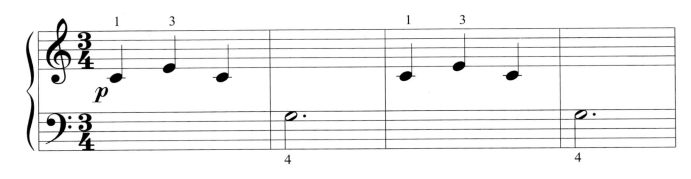

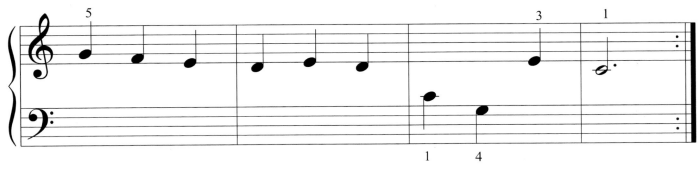

Leaving Gaps in Music

There are signs in music that tell you to leave gaps. These gaps are called *rests*. When you see a rest, count the correct number of beats in your head, before playing the next note.

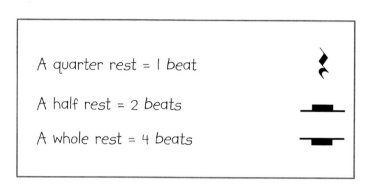

A quarter rest = 1 beat

A half rest = 2 beats

A whole rest = 4 beats

A whole rest is also used to show a rest which lasts for a whole bar.

Missing Beats

All the gaps in this tune have been filled with rests. Count very carefully and remember to lift your fingers off the keys when you see a rest.

You can practice counting this rhythm by clapping the beats. Miss one clap for a quarter rest and two claps for a half rest.

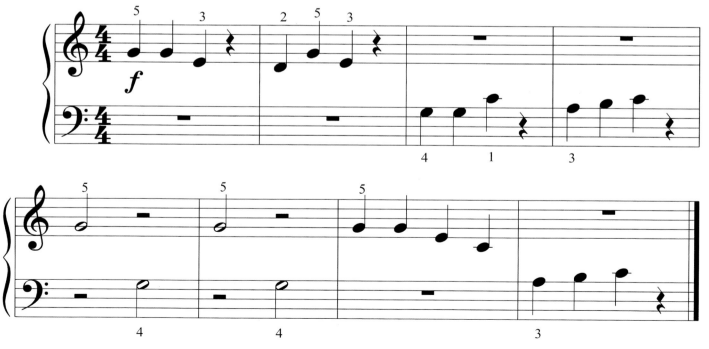

Playing Two Notes at the Same Time

So far you have only played one note at a time. Now you will start playing two notes together. Don't worry if you find it a bit difficult at first. The more you practice, the easier it will become. There are some tips below to help you.

Read the tips below before you try "Double Trouble."

Double Trouble

Practice Hints

- Practice with each hand on its own at first, until you can play both parts without any mistakes.

- When you are sure of the notes, try playing the tune with both hands together.

- Remember to use the correct fingers for each note.

- Start off very slowly, then gradually play the music faster until you are playing at a comfortable speed.

Another Note Length

Here you are going to learn about a shorter note, called an *eighth note*. An eighth note lasts for half a beat. It looks like a quarter note with a tail.

Eighth notes are often joined together in groups of two or four. This makes them easier to read. You can see what they look like below.

These are eighth notes.

This is how two eighth notes are joined together.

This is how four eighth notes are joined together.

Daybreak

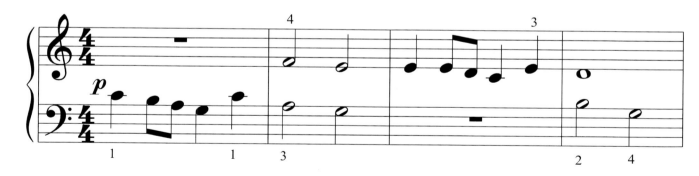

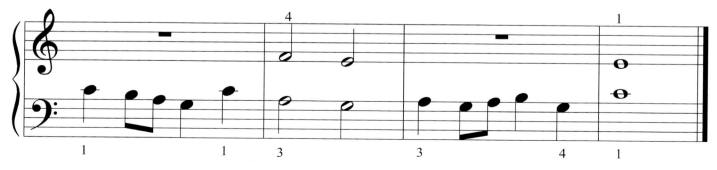

Using the Black Keys

Sometimes the black keys are called *sharp notes,* and sometimes they are called *flat notes.* A sign in front of a note tells you whether it is sharp or flat. A sharp sign in front of a note tells you to press the next key to the right of that note.

This is what a sharp sign looks like. When a note is sharp, it sounds slightly higher.

On the right you can see where to find F sharp on your keyboard.

Middle C

When an F has a sharp sign in front of it, any Fs after it in that bar are also F sharps.

Here you can see how F sharp is written on the staff.

Play F, then F sharp. Can you hear the difference?

Look Sharp!

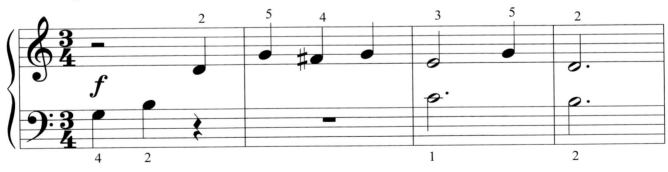

26

A flat sign in front of a note tells you to press the next key to the left of that note. When a note is flat, it sounds slightly lower. On the left you can see what a flat sign looks like. Watch out for the flat signs in "Feeling Flat Blues."

On the right you can see where to find B flat on your keyboard.

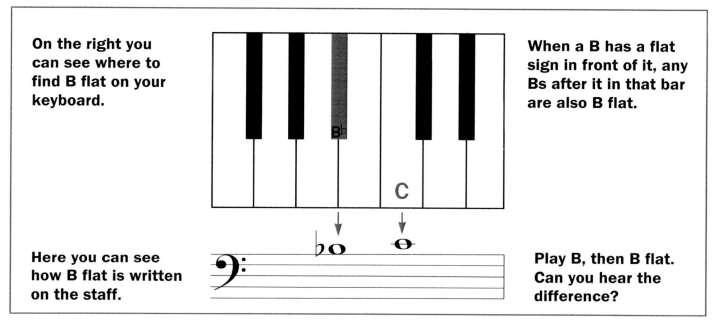

When a B has a flat sign in front of it, any Bs after it in that bar are also B flat.

Here you can see how B flat is written on the staff.

Play B, then B flat. Can you hear the difference?

Feeling Flat Blues

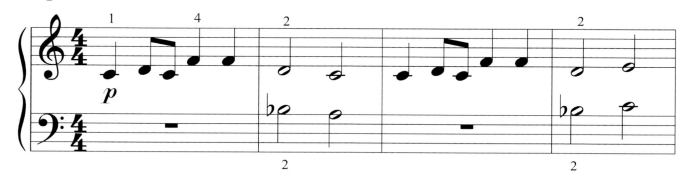

Dotted Quarter Notes

A *dotted quarter note* lasts for one and a half beats. You can see what a dotted quarter note looks like on the right. To play dotted quarter notes, it helps to count "one and two and." Before you play the next tune, try clapping the rhythm.

This is a dotted quarter note.

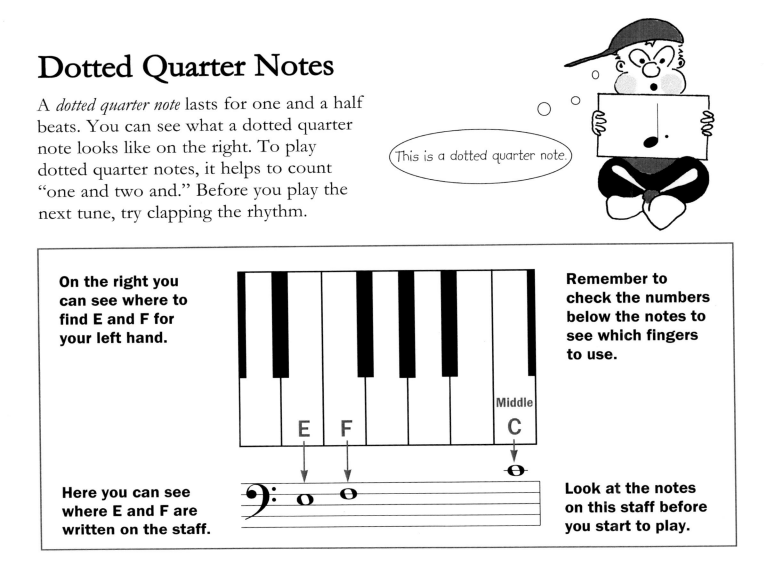

On the right you can see where to find E and F for your left hand.

Here you can see where E and F are written on the staff.

Remember to check the numbers below the notes to see which fingers to use.

Look at the notes on this staff before you start to play.

Summer Song

Count: 1 & 2 & 3 4   1 & 2 & 3 4

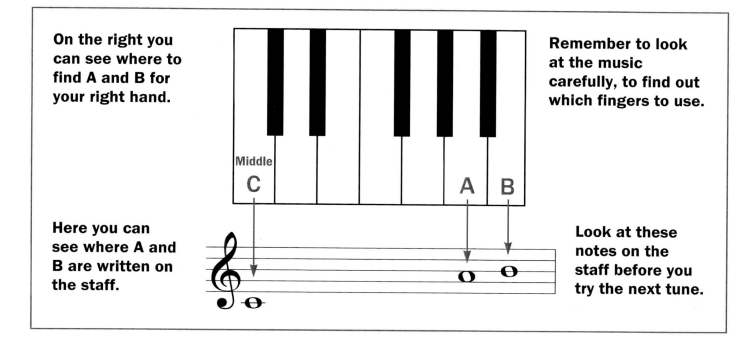

On the right you can see where to find A and B for your right hand.

Remember to look at the music carefully, to find out which fingers to use.

Here you can see where A and B are written on the staff.

Look at these notes on the staff before you try the next tune.

Twinkle, Twinkle, Little Star

Playing Smoothly

The Italian word *legato* tells you to play the music smoothly. Sometimes a curved line, called a slur, tells you to play legato. To play smoothly, press a key and, as you are lifting your finger, begin to press down the next key.

Here you can see where to find D and another note called C for your left hand.

This C sounds lower than Middle C. Play both Cs. Can you hear the difference?

This is how C and D are written on the staff.

Remember to check which fingers to use.

Play the tune below as smoothly as you can.

Frère Jacques

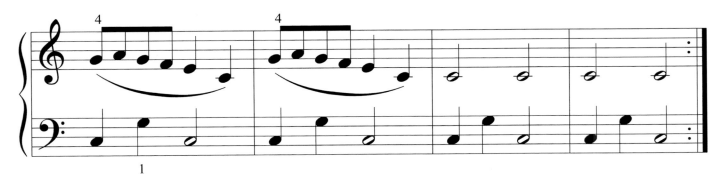

Be careful not to play louder when you play notes staccato.

Another Italian Word

The Italian word *staccato* means "short and detached." A dot above or below a note tells you to play staccato. To play notes staccato, strike the key, then remove your finger as quickly as possible. Try to play staccato notes as short as you can.

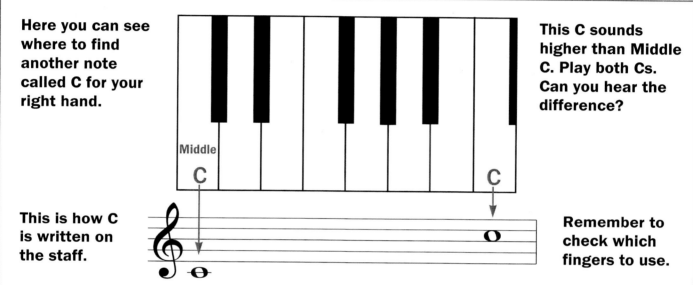

Here you can see where to find another note called C for your right hand.

Middle C

This C sounds higher than Middle C. Play both Cs. Can you hear the difference?

This is how C is written on the staff.

Remember to check which fingers to use.

The Porcupine's Picnic

Congratulations!

Now that you have reached the end of the book, here is a special piece for you play. Practice it until you can play it all the way through without any mistakes. Then you can play it to a friend or relative, to show them what you have learned.

Party Time